C
POEMS
ON THE
UNDERGROUND

edited by
Gerard Benson
Judith Chernaik
Cicely Herbert

CASSELL

Cassell Publishers Limited
Wellington House, 125 Strand
London WC2R 0BB

First published 1996

British Library Cataloguing in Publication Data
A catalogue record for this book is available from the British Library

ISBN 0–304–34807–4

Typeset in Monophoto Meridien by
August Filmsetting, Haydock, St Helens

Printed and bound in Great Britain by
Hillmans Printers Ltd

CONTENTS

THE POEMS

This Is Just to Say

I have eaten
the plums
that were in
the icebox

and which
you were probably
saving
for breakfast

Forgive me
they were delicious
so sweet
and so cold

WILLIAM CARLOS WILLIAMS (1883–1963)

Lady 'Rogue' Singleton

Come, wed me, Lady Singleton,
And we will have a baby soon
And we will live in Edmonton
Where all the friendly people run.

I could never make you happy, darling,
Or give you the baby you want,
I would always very much rather, dear,
Live in a tent.

I am not a cold woman, Henry,
But I do not feel for you,
What I feel for the elephants and the miasmas
And the general view.

STEVIE SMITH (1902–71)

Teeth

English Teeth, English Teeth!
Shining in the sun
A part of British heritage
Aye, each and every one.

English Teeth, Happy Teeth!
Always having fun
Clamping down on bits of fish
And sausages half done.

English Teeth! HEROES' Teeth!
Hear them click! and clack!
Let's sing a song of praise to them –
Three Cheers for the Brown Grey and Black.

SPIKE MILLIGAN (b. 1918)

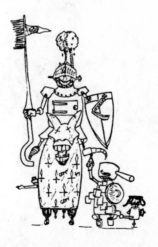

Teeth   Drawing by the Author, in *Silly Verse for Kids* © Spike Milligan,
by permission of Spike Milligan Productions.

Alas, Alack!

Ann, Ann!
  Come! quick as you can!
There's a fish that *talks*
  In the frying-pan.
Out of the fat,
  As clear as glass,
He put up his mouth
  And moaned 'Alas!'
Oh, most mournful,
  'Alas, alack!'
Then turned to his sizzling,
  And sank him back.

WALTER DE LA MARE (1873–1956)

Alas, Alack!   Drawing by W. Heath Robinson, © The Estate of
Mrs J. C. Robinson. By permission of Laurence Pollinger.

The Loch Ness Monster's Song

Sssnnnwhuffffll?
Hnwhuffl hhnnwfl hnfl hfl?
Gdroblboblhobngbl gbl gl g g g g glbgl.
Drublhaflablhaflubhafgabhaflhafl fl fl –
gm grawwwww grf grawf awfgm graw gm.
Hovoplodok-doplodovok-plovodokot-doplodokosh?
Splgraw fok fok splgrafhatchgabrlgabrl fok splfok!
Zgra kra gka fok!
Grof grawff gahf?
Gombl mbl bl –
blm plm,
blm plm,
blm plm,
blp.

EDWIN MORGAN (b. 1920)

'There was an Old Man with a beard'

There was an Old Man with a beard,
Who said, "It is just as I feared! –
　　Two Owls and a Hen,
　　Four Larks and a Wren,
Have all built their nests in my beard!"
from THE BOOK OF NONSENSE

EDWARD LEAR (1812–88)

There was an Old Man with a beard　Drawing by the author, from
The Book of Nonsense.

London Airport

Last night in London Airport
I saw a wooden bin
labelled UNWANTED LITERATURE
IS TO BE PLACED HEREIN.
So I wrote a poem
and popped it in.

CHRISTOPHER LOGUE (b. 1926)

'Sumer is icumen in'

Sumer is icumen in,
Loud sing cuckoo!
Groweth seed and bloweth mead
And springeth the wood now.
Sing cuckoo!

Ewe bleateth after lamb,
Cow loweth after calf,
Bullock starteth, buck farteth,
Merry sing cuckoo!

Cuckoo, cuckoo!
Well singest thou cuckoo,
Nor cease thou never now!

Sing cuckoo now, sing cuckoo!
Sing cuckoo, sing cuckoo now!

ANON. (13th century)

The Leader

I wanna be the leader
I wanna be the leader
Can I be the leader?
Can I? I can?
Promise? Promise?
Yippee, I'm the leader
I'm the leader

OK what shall we do?

ROGER McGOUGH (b. 1937)

London Bells

Two sticks and an apple,
Ring the bells at Whitechapel.

Old Father Bald Pate,
Ring the bells Aldgate.

Maids in white aprons,
Ring the bells at St. Catherine's.

Oranges and lemons,
Ring the bells at St. Clement's.

When will you pay me?
Ring the bells at the Old Bailey.

When I am rich,
Ring the bells at Fleetditch.

When will that be?
Ring the bells at Stepney.

When I am old,
Ring the great bell at Paul's.

ANON. (early 18th century)

London Bells.

Two Sticks и andApple,
Ring ỹ Bells atWhitechapple
Old Father Bald Pate,
Ring ỹ Bells Aldgate,
Maids in white Aprons,
Ring ỹ Bells a St.Cathrines,
Oranges and Lemmons,
Ring ỹ Bells at S.Clemens,
When will you pay me,
Ring ỹ Bells at ỹ OldBailey,
When I am Rich,
Ring ỹ Bells atFleetditch,
When will that be,
Ring ỹ Bells at Stepney,
When I am Old,
Ring ỹgreat Bell at Pauls.

London Bells   The traditional London rhyme as it appears in an early
hand-set printed children's book, *Tommy Thumb's Pretty Song Book* (1744),
Vol. II. By permission of The British Library Board.

Sergeant Brown's Parrot

Many policemen wear upon their shoulders
Cunning little radios. To pass away the time
They talk about the traffic to them, listen to the news,
And it helps them to Keep Down Crime.

But Sergeant Brown, he wears upon his shoulder
A tall green parrot as he's walking up and down
And all the parrot says is "Who's-a-pretty-boy-then?"
"I am," says Sergeant Brown.

KIT WRIGHT (b. 1944)

Sergeant Brown's Parrot   Drawing by Posy Simmonds,
© Posy Simmonds. By permission of Collins Publishers.

'I have a gentil cock'

I have a gentil cock
   croweth me day
he doth me risen early
   my matins for to say

I have a gentil cock
   comen he is of great
his comb is of red coral
   his tail is of jet

I have a gentil cock
   comen he is of kind
his comb is of red sorrel
   his tail is of inde

his legs be of azure
   so gentil and so small
his spurs are of silver white
   into the wortewale

his eyes are of crystal
   locked all in amber
and every night he percheth him
   in my lady's chamber

ANON. (early 15th century)

I saw a Jolly Hunter

I saw a jolly hunter
With a jolly gun
Walking in the country
In the jolly sun.

In the jolly meadow
Sat a jolly hare.
Saw the jolly hunter.
Took jolly care.

Hunter jolly eager –
Sight of jolly prey.
Forgot gun pointing
Wrong jolly way.

Jolly hunter jolly head
Over heels gone.
Jolly old safety catch
Not jolly on.

Bang went the jolly gun.
Hunter jolly dead.
Jolly hare got clean away.
Jolly good, I said.

CHARLES CAUSLEY (b. 1917)

I saw a Jolly Hunter Drawing by
Pat Marriott, from *Figgie Hobbin*.
By permission of Macmillan London.

Old English Riddle

A moth, I thought, munching a word.
How marvellously weird! a worm
Digesting a man's sayings –
A sneakthief nibbling in the shadows
At the shape of a poet's thunderous phrases –
How unutterably strange!
And the pilfering parasite none the wiser
For the words he has swallowed.

from THE EXETER BOOK
translated by GERARD BENSON

Answer: Bookworm

The Cries of London

Here's fine rosemary, sage, and thyme.
Come buy my ground ivy.
Here's fetherfew, gilliflowers and rue.
Come buy my knotted marjorum, ho!
Come buy my mint, my fine green mint.
Here's fine lavender for your cloaths.
Here's parsley and winter-savory,
And hearts-ease, which all do choose.
Here's balm and hissop, and cinquefoil,
All fine herbs, it is well known.
    Let none despise the merry, merry cries
    Of famous London-town!

Here's fine herrings, eight a groat.
Hot codlins, pies and tarts.
New mackerel! have to sell.
Come buy my Wellfleet oysters, ho!
Come buy my whitings fine and new.
Wives, shall I mend your husbands horns?
I'll grind your knives to please your wives,
And very nicely cut your corns.
Maids, have you any hair to sell,
Either flaxen, black, or brown?
    Let none despise the merry, merry cries
    Of famous London-town!

ANON. (17th century)

The Uncertainty of the Poet

I am a poet.
I am very fond of bananas.

I am bananas.
I am very fond of a poet.

I am a poet of bananas.
I am very fond.

A fond poet of 'I am, I am' –
Very bananas.

Fond of 'Am I bananas?
Am I?' – a very poet.

Bananas of a poet!
Am I fond? Am I very?

Poet bananas! I am.
I am fond of a 'very'.

I am of very fond bananas.
Am I a poet?

WENDY COPE (b. 1945)

'I saw a Peacock with a fiery tail'

I saw a Peacock with a fiery tail
I saw a blazing Comet drop down hail
I saw a Cloud with Ivy circled round
I saw a sturdy Oak creep on the ground
I saw a Pismire swallow up a Whale
I saw a raging Sea brim full of Ale
I saw a Venice Glass sixteen foot deep
I saw a Well full of men's tears that weep
I saw their Eyes all in a flame of fire
I saw a House as big as the Moon and higher
I saw the Sun even in the midst of night
I saw the Man that saw this wondrous sight.

ANON. (17th century)

A song for England

An' a so de rain a-fall
An' a so de snow a-rain

An' a so de fog a-fall
An' a so de sun a-fail

An' a so de seasons mix
An' a so de bag-o'-tricks

But a so me understan'
De misery o' de Englishman.

ANDREW SALKEY (1928–95)

The Lobster Quadrille

'Will you walk a little faster?' said a whiting to a snail,
'There's a porpoise close behind us, and he's treading on my tail.
See how eagerly the lobsters and the turtles all advance!
They are waiting on the shingle – will you come and join the dance?
  Will you, won't you, will you, won't you,
    Will you join the dance?
  Will you, won't you, will you, won't you,
    Won't you join the dance?

'You can really have no notion how delightful it will be
When they take us up and throw us, with the lobsters, out to sea!'
But the snail replied 'Too far, too far!', and gave a look askance –
Said he thanked the whiting kindly, but he would not join the dance.
  Would not, could not, would not, could not,
    Would not join the dance.
  Would not, could not, would not, could not,
    Could not join the dance.

'What matters it how far we go?' his scaly friend replied.
'There is another shore, you know, upon the other side.
The further off from England the nearer is to France –
Then turn not pale, beloved snail, but come and join the dance.
  Will you, won't you, will you, won't you,
    Will you join the dance?
  Will you, won't you, will you, won't you,
    Won't you join the dance?'

LEWIS CARROLL (1832–98)

The Lobster Quadrille   Illustration by John Tenniel.

To Someone Who Insisted I Look Up Someone

I rang them up while touring Timbuctoo,
Those bosom chums to whom you're known as *'Who?'*

X. J. KENNEDY (b. 1929)

The Flaw in Paganism

Drink and dance and laugh and lie,
    Love, the reeling midnight through,
For tomorrow we shall die!
    (But, alas, we never do.)

DOROTHY PARKER (1893–1967)

The Algonquin Round Table   Dorothy Parker (lower left) surrounded by
Robert Benchley, Alfred Lunt and Lynn Fontanne, Frank Crowninshield,
Alexander Woollcott, Heywood Broun, Marc Connelly, Frank Case,
Franklin P. Adams, Edna Ferber, George Kaufman and Robert Sherwood.
Illustration by Al Hirschfeld.

A True and Faithful Inventory
of the Goods *belonging* to Dr. Swift,
Vicar of *Lara Cor*;
upon lending his House to the Bishop of Meath,
until his own was built

An Oaken, broken, Elbow-Chair;
A Cawdle-Cup, without an Ear;
A batter'd, shatter'd Ash Bedstead;
A Box of Deal, without a Lid;
A Pair of Tongs, but out of Joint;
A Back-Sword Poker, without Point;
A Pot that's crack'd across, around,
With an old knotted Garter bound;
An Iron Lock, without a Key;
A Wig, with hanging, quite grown grey;
A Curtain worn to Half a Stripe;
A Pair of Bellows, without Pipe;
A Dish, which might good Meat afford once;
An *Ovid*, and an old *Concordance*;
A Bottle Bottom, Wooden Platter,
One is for Meal, and one for Water:
There likewise is a Copper Skillet,
Which runs as fast out as you fill it;
A Candlestick, Snuff dish, and Save-all,
And thus his Household Goods you have all.
These, to your Lordship, as a Friend,
Till you have built, I freely lend:
They'll save your Lordship for a Shift;
Why not, as well as Doctor *Swift*?

THOMAS SHERIDAN (1687–1738)

Sun a-shine, rain a-fall

Sun a-shine an' rain a-fall,
The Devil an' him wife cyan 'gree at all,
The two o' them want one fish-head,
The Devil call him wife bonehead,
She hiss her teeth, call him cock-eye,
Greedy, worthless an' workshy,
While them busy callin' name,
The puss walk in, sey is a shame
To see a nice fish go to was'e,
Lef' with a big grin pon him face.

VALERIE BLOOM (b. 1956)

Sun a-shine, rain a-fall   Illustration by Michael Charlton.

ACKNOWLEDGEMENTS

Gerard Benson: 'Old English Riddle', © Gerard Benson 1990. Reprinted by permission of the author.

Valerie Bloom: 'Sun a-shine, rain a-fall' from *Duppy Jamboree* (1992) © Cambridge University Press. Reprinted by permission of Cambridge University Press.

Charles Causley: 'I Saw a Jolly Hunter' from *Figgie Hobbin* © Charles Causley 1970. Reprinted by permission of Macmillan Publishers and David Higham Associates.

Wendy Cope: 'The Uncertainty of the Poet' from *With a Poet's Eye: A Tate Gallery Anthology* (1986), © Wendy Cope 1986. By permission of Faber and Faber.

Walter de la Mare: 'Alas, Alack!' from *Peacock Pie*. Reprinted by permission of The Literary Trustees of Walter de la Mare and The Society of Authors as their representative.

X. J. Kennedy: 'To Someone Who Insisted I Look Up Someone' from *Cross Ties: Selected Poems* (1985), © X. J. Kennedy 1985. Reprinted by permission of Curtis Brown, New York.

Christopher Logue: 'London Airport' from *Ode to the Dodo. Poems 1953–1978* by Christopher Logue, © Christopher Logue 1981. Reprinted by permission of Faber and Faber.

Roger McGough: 'The Leader' from *Sky in the Pie* (Kestrel) © Roger McGough 1983. Reprinted by permission of Peters, Fraser & Dunlop.

Spike Milligan: 'Teeth' from *Silly Verse for Kids*, Puffin Books, © Spike Milligan 1959, 1961, 1963. Reprinted by permission of Spike Milligan Productions.

Edwin Morgan: 'The Loch Ness Monster's Song' from *Collected Poems*, © Edwin Morgan 1990. Reprinted by permission of Carcanet Press.

Dorothy Parker: 'The Flaw in Paganism', from *The Collected Dorothy Parker*, © The Estate of Dorothy Parker 1973. Reprinted by permission of Duckworth and Viking.

Andrew Salkey: 'A Song for England' from *Caribbean Voices 2*, ed. John Figueroa (1970), © Andrew Salkey. Reprinted by permission of the author's Estate.

Stevie Smith: 'Lady "Rogue" Singleton' from *The Collected Poems of Stevie Smith* (Penguin 20th Century Classics), © Stevie Smith 1972. Reprinted by permission of the Executor, James MacGibbon.

William Carlos Williams: 'This Is Just to Say' from *The Collected Poems 1909–39*, ed. A. Walton Litz and Christopher MacGowan. Reprinted by permission of Carcanet Press.

Kit Wright: 'Sergeant Brown's Parrot' from *Rabbiting On*, © Kit Wright 1978. Reprinted by permission of HarperCollins Publishers.

'Poems on the Underground' wish to thank London Underground Ltd, London Arts Board, the British Council and the Stefan Zweig Programme of The British Library. Posters of poems displayed on the Underground can be purchased from the London Transport Museum, Freepost, Covent Garden, London WC2E 7BB.